CI

MW01076451

The Guitar Practice Journal

Organise your practice, track your progress and become a better guitar player

In this book is 52 weeks worth of practice log sheets. Under each week you are able to keep track of what you're working on, note down problem areas and successes, focus on the areas to improve and pick up your practice the following week from exactly where you left off the week before. There is space to record your best speeds for the scales you are working on as well as how long you have spent practicing each day meaning that you are able to see exactly how effective your practice has been. At the beginning of the book you also have the opportunity to write your monthly and yearly goals so that you can compare your weekly progress against your longer term aims.

The Old Bank
77 Railway Road
Brinscall
Lancashire
UK
PR6 8RJ

www.alexdansonmusic.com

Written by Alex Danson
Cover Designed by Caroline Håkansson

Using this book

1. Set realistic yet challenging goals

Having goals which stretch your ability yet are within reach is extremely important in keeping your motivation at a maximum. You need to be able to see yourself achieving the goals you set for yourself and you also need to be excited about the prospect. Constantly review your goals and check your progress against them as you go along. You may need to adjust them and make them easier or more difficult to attain as you progress so don't set them in stone.

2. Be honest

You will get the most out of this book if you are honest towards yourself. For example, your best speed on the warm up exercises and scales is the highest speed at which you can consistently play the exercise or scale without making a mistake. Don't rush to up the speed. Take your time, be accurate and bed in good technique. The time spent practicing is another section which requires honesty in order for it to be effective in keeping up your discipline.

3. Be critical

If you are learning a song and there is one section which isn't sounding quite right, make a note of it and work on it during the next week. The chances are the techniques or chords used in that section will come up again in another song later on down the line so it's worth spending the time to get it right.

4. But don't be too critical

There's no need to go over the top on self criticism. If you are finding a song, solo or technique particularly difficult then don't take it to heart. Break it down into sections and spread it out over a few practice sessions or set it for yourself a few weeks down the line after you've laid down some more groundwork. The aim is to make small improvements as you go along so don't try to take on too much at once.

5. Keep it fun

Don't put too much pressure on yourself with regards to how much time you spend practicing. Playing guitar should remain fun and not a chore. Practice more when the mood strikes but if you find yourself getting bored or frustrated, put the guitar down for a while and come back later with a fresh head. Short, concentrated bursts are often very effective and leave you wanting more!

Guitar Playing Goals

This year's goals	
Month 1	
Month 2	
Month 3	
Month 4	
Month 5	
Month 6	
Month 7	
Month 8	
Month 9	
Month 10	
Month 11	
Month 12	

Week 1

Warm ups and scales	Notes	Best speed (beats per minute)

New chords	Notes

Songs / Riffs / Solos	Notes

Techniques / Technical exercises	Notes

Extras	Notes

Practice summary, problem points and successes

Day	Mon	Tues	Weds	Thurs	Fri	Sat	Sun
Time Spent							

Week 2

Warm ups and scales	Notes	Best speed (beats per minute)

New chords	Notes

Songs / Riffs / Solos	Notes

Techniques / Technical exercises	Notes

Extras	Notes

Practice summary, problem points and successes

Day	Mon	Tues	Weds	Thurs	Fri	Sat	Sun
Time Spent							

Week 3

Warm ups and scales	Notes	Best speed (beats per minute)

New chords	Notes

Songs / Riffs / Solos	Notes

Techniques / Technical exercises	Notes

Extras	Notes

Practice summary, problem points and successes

Day	Mon	Tues	Weds	Thurs	Fri	Sat	Sun
Time Spent							

Week 4

Warm ups and scales	Notes	Best speed (beats per minute)

New chords	Notes

Songs / Riffs / Solos	Notes

Techniques / Technical exercises	Notes

Extras	Notes

Practice summary, problem points and successes

Day	Mon	Tues	Weds	Thurs	Fri	Sat	Sun
Time Spent							

Week 5

Warm ups and scales	Notes	Best speed (beats per minute)

New chords	Notes

Songs / Riffs / Solos	Notes

Techniques / Technical exercises	Notes

Extras	Notes

Practice summary, problem points and successes

Day	Mon	Tues	Weds	Thurs	Fri	Sat	Sun
Time Spent							

Week 6

Warm ups and scales	Notes	Best speed (beats per minute)

New chords	Notes

Songs / Riffs / Solos	Notes

Techniques / Technical exercises	Notes

Extras	Notes

Practice summary, problem points and successes

Day	Mon	Tues	Weds	Thurs	Fri	Sat	Sun
Time Spent							

Week 7

Warm ups and scales	Notes	Best speed (beats per minute)

New chords	Notes

Songs / Riffs / Solos	Notes

Techniques / Technical exercises	Notes

Extras	Notes

Practice summary, problem points and successes

Day	Mon	Tues	Weds	Thurs	Fri	Sat	Sun
Time Spent							

Week 8

Warm ups and scales	Notes	Best speed (beats per minute)

New chords	Notes

Songs / Riffs / Solos	Notes

Techniques / Technical exercises	Notes

Extras	Notes

Practice summary, problem points and successes

Day	Mon	Tues	Weds	Thurs	Fri	Sat	Sun
Time Spent							

Week 9

Warm ups and scales	Notes	Best speed (beats per minute)

New chords	Notes

Songs / Riffs / Solos	Notes

Techniques / Technical exercises	Notes

Extras	Notes

Practice summary, problem points and successes

Day	Mon	Tues	Weds	Thurs	Fri	Sat	Sun
Time Spent							

Week 10

Warm ups and scales	Notes	Best speed (beats per minute)

New chords	Notes

Songs / Riffs / Solos	Notes

Techniques / Technical exercises	Notes

Extras	Notes

Practice summary, problem points and successes

Day	Mon	Tues	Weds	Thurs	Fri	Sat	Sun
Time Spent							

Week 11

Warm ups and scales	Notes	Best speed (beats per minute)

New chords	Notes

Songs / Riffs / Solos	Notes

Techniques / Technical exercises	Notes

Extras	Notes

Practice summary, problem points and successes

Day	Mon	Tues	Weds	Thurs	Fri	Sat	Sun
Time Spent							

Week 12

Warm ups and scales	Notes	Best speed (beats per minute)

New chords	Notes

Songs / Riffs / Solos	Notes

Techniques / Technical exercises	Notes

Extras	Notes

Practice summary, problem points and successes

Day	Mon	Tues	Weds	Thurs	Fri	Sat	Sun
Time Spent							

Week 13

Warm ups and scales	Notes	Best speed (beats per minute)

New chords	Notes

Songs / Riffs / Solos	Notes

Techniques / Technical exercises	Notes

Extras	Notes

Practice summary, problem points and successes

Day	Mon	Tues	Weds	Thurs	Fri	Sat	Sun
Time Spent							

Week 14

Warm ups and scales	Notes	Best speed (beats per minute)

New chords	Notes

Songs / Riffs / Solos	Notes

Techniques / Technical exercises	Notes

Extras	Notes

Practice summary, problem points and successes

Day	Mon	Tues	Weds	Thurs	Fri	Sat	Sun
Time Spent							

Week 15

Warm ups and scales	Notes	Best speed (beats per minute)

New chords	Notes

Songs / Riffs / Solos	Notes

Techniques / Technical exercises	Notes

Extras	Notes

Practice summary, problem points and successes

Day	Mon	Tues	Weds	Thurs	Fri	Sat	Sun
Time Spent							

Week 16

Warm ups and scales	Notes	Best speed (beats per minute)

New chords	Notes

Songs / Riffs / Solos	Notes

Techniques / Technical exercises	Notes

Extras	Notes

Practice summary, problem points and successes

Day	Mon	Tues	Weds	Thurs	Fri	Sat	Sun
Time Spent							

Week 17

Warm ups and scales	Notes	Best speed (beats per minute)

New chords	Notes

Songs / Riffs / Solos	Notes

Techniques / Technical exercises	Notes

Extras	Notes

Practice summary, problem points and successes

Day	Mon	Tues	Weds	Thurs	Fri	Sat	Sun
Time Spent							

Week 18

Warm ups and scales	Notes	Best speed (beats per minute)

New chords	Notes

Songs / Riffs / Solos	Notes

Techniques / Technical exercises	Notes

Extras	Notes

Practice summary, problem points and successes

Day	Mon	Tues	Weds	Thurs	Fri	Sat	Sun
Time Spent							

Week 19

Warm ups and scales	Notes	Best speed (beats per minute)

New chords	Notes

Songs / Riffs / Solos	Notes

Techniques / Technical exercises	Notes

Extras	Notes

Practice summary, problem points and successes

Day	Mon	Tues	Weds	Thurs	Fri	Sat	Sun
Time Spent							

Week 20

Warm ups and scales	Notes	Best speed (beats per minute)

New chords	Notes

Songs / Riffs / Solos	Notes

Techniques / Technical exercises	Notes

Extras	Notes

Practice summary, problem points and successes

Day	Mon	Tues	Weds	Thurs	Fri	Sat	Sun
Time Spent							

Week 21

Warm ups and scales	Notes	Best speed (beats per minute)

New chords	Notes

Songs / Riffs / Solos	Notes

Techniques / Technical exercises	Notes

Extras	Notes

Practice summary, problem points and successes

Day	Mon	Tues	Weds	Thurs	Fri	Sat	Sun
Time Spent							

Week 22

Warm ups and scales	Notes	Best speed (beats per minute)

New chords	Notes

Songs / Riffs / Solos	Notes

Techniques / Technical exercises	Notes

Extras	Notes

Practice summary, problem points and successes

Day	Mon	Tues	Weds	Thurs	Fri	Sat	Sun
Time Spent							

Week 23

Warm ups and scales	Notes	Best speed (beats per minute)

New chords	Notes

Songs / Riffs / Solos	Notes

Techniques / Technical exercises	Notes

Extras	Notes

Practice summary, problem points and successes

Day	Mon	Tues	Weds	Thurs	Fri	Sat	Sun
Time Spent							

Week 24

Warm ups and scales	Notes	Best speed (beats per minute)

New chords	Notes

Songs / Riffs / Solos	Notes

Techniques / Technical exercises	Notes

Extras	Notes

Practice summary, problem points and successes

Day	Mon	Tues	Weds	Thurs	Fri	Sat	Sun
Time Spent							

Week 25

Warm ups and scales	Notes	Best speed (beats per minute)

New chords	Notes

Songs / Riffs / Solos	Notes

Techniques / Technical exercises	Notes

Extras	Notes

Practice summary, problem points and successes

Day	Mon	Tues	Weds	Thurs	Fri	Sat	Sun
Time Spent							

Week 26

Warm ups and scales	Notes	Best speed (beats per minute)

New chords	Notes

Songs / Riffs / Solos	Notes

Techniques / Technical exercises	Notes

Extras	Notes

Practice summary, problem points and successes

Day	Mon	Tues	Weds	Thurs	Fri	Sat	Sun
Time Spent							

Week 27

Warm ups and scales	Notes	Best speed (beats per minute)

New chords	Notes

Songs / Riffs / Solos	Notes

Techniques / Technical exercises	Notes

Extras	Notes

Practice summary, problem points and successes

Day	Mon	Tues	Weds	Thurs	Fri	Sat	Sun
Time Spent							

Week 28

Warm ups and scales	Notes	Best speed (beats per minute)

New chords	Notes

Songs / Riffs / Solos	Notes

Techniques / Technical exercises	Notes

Extras	Notes

Practice summary, problem points and successes

Day	Mon	Tues	Weds	Thurs	Fri	Sat	Sun
Time Spent							

Week 29

Warm ups and scales	Notes	Best speed (beats per minute)

New chords	Notes

Songs / Riffs / Solos	Notes

Techniques / Technical exercises	Notes

Extras	Notes

Practice summary, problem points and successes

Day	Mon	Tues	Weds	Thurs	Fri	Sat	Sun
Time Spent							

Week 30

Warm ups and scales	Notes	Best speed (beats per minute)

New chords	Notes

Songs / Riffs / Solos	Notes

Techniques / Technical exercises	Notes

Extras	Notes

Practice summary, problem points and successes

Day	Mon	Tues	Weds	Thurs	Fri	Sat	Sun
Time Spent							

Week 31

Warm ups and scales	Notes	Best speed (beats per minute)

New chords	Notes

Songs / Riffs / Solos	Notes

Techniques / Technical exercises	Notes

Extras	Notes

Practice summary, problem points and successes

Day	Mon	Tues	Weds	Thurs	Fri	Sat	Sun
Time Spent							

Week 32

Warm ups and scales	Notes	Best speed (beats per minute)

New chords	Notes

Songs / Riffs / Solos	Notes

Techniques / Technical exercises	Notes

Extras	Notes

Practice summary, problem points and successes

Day	Mon	Tues	Weds	Thurs	Fri	Sat	Sun
Time Spent							

Week 33

Warm ups and scales	Notes	Best speed (beats per minute)

New chords	Notes

Songs / Riffs / Solos	Notes

Techniques / Technical exercises	Notes

Extras	Notes

Practice summary, problem points and successes

Day	Mon	Tues	Weds	Thurs	Fri	Sat	Sun
Time Spent							

Week 34

Warm ups and scales	Notes	Best speed (beats per minute)

New chords	Notes

Songs / Riffs / Solos	Notes

Techniques / Technical exercises	Notes

Extras	Notes

Practice summary, problem points and successes

Day	Mon	Tues	Weds	Thurs	Fri	Sat	Sun
Time Spent							

Week 35

Warm ups and scales	Notes	Best speed (beats per minute)

New chords	Notes

Songs / Riffs / Solos	Notes

Techniques / Technical exercises	Notes

Extras	Notes

Practice summary, problem points and successes

Day	Mon	Tues	Weds	Thurs	Fri	Sat	Sun
Time Spent							

Week 36

Warm ups and scales	Notes	Best speed (beats per minute)

New chords	Notes

Songs / Riffs / Solos	Notes

Techniques / Technical exercises	Notes

Extras	Notes

Practice summary, problem points and successes

Day	Mon	Tues	Weds	Thurs	Fri	Sat	Sun
Time Spent							

Week 37

Warm ups and scales	Notes	Best speed (beats per minute)

New chords	Notes

Songs / Riffs / Solos	Notes

Techniques / Technical exercises	Notes

Extras	Notes

Practice summary, problem points and successes

Day	Mon	Tues	Weds	Thurs	Fri	Sat	Sun
Time Spent							

Week 38

Warm ups and scales	Notes	Best speed (beats per minute)

New chords	Notes

Songs / Riffs / Solos	Notes

Techniques / Technical exercises	Notes

Extras	Notes

Practice summary, problem points and successes

Day	Mon	Tues	Weds	Thurs	Fri	Sat	Sun
Time Spent							

Week 39

Warm ups and scales	Notes	Best speed (beats per minute)

New chords	Notes

Songs / Riffs / Solos	Notes

Techniques / Technical exercises	Notes

Extras	Notes

Practice summary, problem points and successes

Day	Mon	Tues	Weds	Thurs	Fri	Sat	Sun
Time Spent							

Week 40

Warm ups and scales	Notes	Best speed (beats per minute)

New chords	Notes

Songs / Riffs / Solos	Notes

Techniques / Technical exercises	Notes

Extras	Notes

Practice summary, problem points and successes

Day	Mon	Tues	Weds	Thurs	Fri	Sat	Sun
Time Spent							

Week 41

Warm ups and scales	Notes	Best speed (beats per minute)

New chords	Notes

Songs / Riffs / Solos	Notes

Techniques / Technical exercises	Notes

Extras	Notes

Practice summary, problem points and successes

Day	Mon	Tues	Weds	Thurs	Fri	Sat	Sun
Time Spent							

Week 42

Warm ups and scales	Notes	Best speed (beats per minute)

New chords	Notes

Songs / Riffs / Solos	Notes

Techniques / Technical exercises	Notes

Extras	Notes

Practice summary, problem points and successes

Day	Mon	Tues	Weds	Thurs	Fri	Sat	Sun
Time Spent							

Week 43

Warm ups and scales	Notes	Best speed (beats per minute)

New chords	Notes

Songs / Riffs / Solos	Notes

Techniques / Technical exercises	Notes

Extras	Notes

Practice summary, problem points and successes

Day	Mon	Tues	Weds	Thurs	Fri	Sat	Sun
Time Spent							

Week 44

Warm ups and scales	Notes	Best speed (beats per minute)

New chords	Notes

Songs / Riffs / Solos	Notes

Techniques / Technical exercises	Notes

Extras	Notes

Practice summary, problem points and successes

Day	Mon	Tues	Weds	Thurs	Fri	Sat	Sun
Time Spent							

Week 45

Warm ups and scales	Notes	Best speed (beats per minute)

New chords	Notes

Songs / Riffs / Solos	Notes

Techniques / Technical exercises	Notes

Extras	Notes

Practice summary, problem points and successes

Day	Mon	Tues	Weds	Thurs	Fri	Sat	Sun
Time Spent							

Week 46

Warm ups and scales	Notes	Best speed (beats per minute)

New chords	Notes

Songs / Riffs / Solos	Notes

Techniques / Technical exercises	Notes

Extras	Notes

Practice summary, problem points and successes

Day	Mon	Tues	Weds	Thurs	Fri	Sat	Sun
Time Spent							

Week 47

Warm ups and scales	Notes	Best speed (beats per minute)

New chords	Notes

Songs / Riffs / Solos	Notes

Techniques / Technical exercises	Notes

Extras	Notes

Practice summary, problem points and successes

Day	Mon	Tues	Weds	Thurs	Fri	Sat	Sun
Time Spent							

Week 48

Warm ups and scales	Notes	Best speed (beats per minute)

New chords	Notes

Songs / Riffs / Solos	Notes

Techniques / Technical exercises	Notes

Extras	Notes

Practice summary, problem points and successes

Day	Mon	Tues	Weds	Thurs	Fri	Sat	Sun
Time Spent							

Week 49

Warm ups and scales	Notes	Best speed (beats per minute)

New chords	Notes

Songs / Riffs / Solos	Notes

Techniques / Technical exercises	Notes

Extras	Notes

Practice summary, problem points and successes

Day	Mon	Tues	Weds	Thurs	Fri	Sat	Sun
Time Spent							

Week 50

Warm ups and scales	Notes	Best speed (beats per minute)

New chords	Notes

Songs / Riffs / Solos	Notes

Techniques / Technical exercises	Notes

Extras	Notes

Practice summary, problem points and successes

Day	Mon	Tues	Weds	Thurs	Fri	Sat	Sun
Time Spent							

Week 51

Warm ups and scales	Notes	Best speed (beats per minute)

New chords	Notes

Songs / Riffs / Solos	Notes

Techniques / Technical exercises	Notes

Extras	Notes

Practice summary, problem points and successes

Day	Mon	Tues	Weds	Thurs	Fri	Sat	Sun
Time Spent							

Week 52

Warm ups and scales	Notes	Best speed (beats per minute)

New chords	Notes

Songs / Riffs / Solos	Notes

Techniques / Technical exercises	Notes

Extras	Notes

Practice summary, problem points and successes

Day	Mon	Tues	Weds	Thurs	Fri	Sat	Sun
Time Spent							

About Clearwater Music School

Clearwater Music School is based in the heart of rural Lancashire, North West England, and was set up by Alex Danson in 2013. The music school offers lessons in guitar, singing, piano, keyboard, bass guitar, ukulele and more.

Alex has started producing these books as an extension to Clearwater Music School and to provide useful resources for music learners of all types around the world.

Visit **www.clearwatermusic.co.uk** for more information on the music school.

Visit **www.alexdansonmusic.com** to find out more information about Alex.

Further Titles

Simply Guitar Tab

Simply Guitar Tab with Traditional Music Notation

Simply Chord Diagrams

Simply Sheet Music

Simply Bass Guitar Tab

Simply Ukulele Tab

Coming Soon

The Essential Scale Handbook for Guitarists

There are many more books and resources on the way which will be available on Amazon and from Clearwater Music School directly.

To stay up to date with releases - visit **alexdansonmusic.com** and subscribe to the email list.

Made in the USA
Lexington, KY
19 March 2015